Kuɛ̈nɛ Kɛ Thök
Nuer Nyatöng Duop

Daniel Gatluak P. Well

Rev. date: 12/05/2013

To order additional copies of this book, contact:
Xlibris LLC
1-888-795-4274
www.Xlibris.com
Orders@Xlibris.com

Kuene ke thok Nath Bok Kel
Meaning reading in Nuer dialect Book One

BANI THOK NATH

A	Ɛ	I	Ö	U
W	Y	B	P	M
N	NH	Ŋ	NY	R
D	DH	T	TH	L
K	G	Ɣ	C	J
Ɛ	Ä	Ɔ	O	

NUER

Malɛ gaat South Sudanese Americans

Malɛ Mi gua ɛ baba
Male kɛ Run-waŋ gaat baba
Malɛ mi guɔä baba
Malɛ kɛ cäŋ gaat baba
Malɛ mi guɔa baba
Malɛ kɛ thiaŋ gaat baba
Malɛ mi guɔä baba
Malɛ kɛ wäär gaat baba
Malɛ mi guɔä baba

ENGLISH

Greeting to all of you south Sudanese Americans children
Greeting to you father
Good morning to you my children
Greeting father
Good afternoon my children
Greeting father
Good evening my children
Greeting to you father
How are you tonight children
We are find thank Father

Gaat Nuer: Ti ti kɛ Gaat Nuer daŋ rew kɛ Greater upper Nile State South Sudan.
English: This two Nuer boys are from Upper Nile State in South Sudan.
Nuer: Dhöli duɛl-gɔrä ci kɛ nyuor duɛl-gcrä kɛ upper Nile State.

NUER		ENGLISH
Bɛl	meaning	Nuer traditional melted for food
Bul	meaning	Drum for playing weding party or it is for church parying during singing
Bith	meaning	sword it is use for fishing
Cuk	meaning	pot it is hand made from mud careing cool drinking water
Ciik	meaning	more pots for caring drinking waters
Cäl	meaning	cat fish
Dɛt	meaning	goat
Dit	meaning	bird
Döw	meaning	little cow baby
Dhaar	meaning	cooking pot or pot to keep cooler drinking water
Dhool	meaning	Nuer Boy from age 7, upto 18 years of age
Dhäŋ	meaning	Nuer hand made sleeping bed
Rɛc	meaning	cat fish, very special fish in south Sudan from Nuer Land
Guɛc	meaning	tall animal call Drafts
Duɛl	meaning	Nuer Traditional house. In south Sudan
Dɛl	meaning	Nuer goat at South Sudan
Lɛk	meaning	Nuer hand made traditional food making
Rec	meaning	cat fishes
Göök	meaning	monkey
Gumut	meaning	One of South Sudanese Bird call Gumut
Gat	meaning	child
ɣɔ_k	meaning	Cows
ɣʊth	meaning	one of Nuer Traditional Food caring
ɣök	meaning	Nuer hand made water caring for cool drinking water
Pil	meaning	one of Nuer Traditional food making
Rip	meaning	one of Nuer hand making
Tic	meaning	one of Nuer traditional house at south Sudanese

Jith	meaning	one of South Sudanese insects
Jöp	meaning	0xis
Jiök	meaning	Dog
Kun	meaning	rate
Kɛɛt	meaning	strike
Kölög	meaning	puger pip
Löny	meaning	lion
Law	meaning	Nuer Traditional hand made for boat use
Lɛl	meaning	Nuer traditional hand made
Mut	meaning	Nuer Traditional sword for hunting for South Sudanese men in the villages
Mök	meaning	one of the animal in South Sudanese
Mänytap	meaning	corn
Naath	meaning	people
Närmuon	meaning	one insect in South Sudanese
Nör	meaning	one of crook ding net in South Sudanese
Nhiääl	meaning	rain
Nhiäc	meaning	ring water out, from wet clothes
Nyän	meaning	corroding
Nyäl	meaning	Nuer young girl at south Sudanese in Africa
Nyöngol	meaning	this is the bird call nyongol from south Sudanese
Nöm	meaning	the Nuer hand made for cutting the meat
Näp	meaning	one of the smaller bird which stray some time in the house
ɣök	meaning	cutting for anything
Gön	meaning	group of bird call gon in south Sudanese
Thom	meaning	one of south Sudanese hand made music for playing
Bok	meaning	Nuer Book for Nuer Language
Kom	meaning	Nuer chair for sitting in south Sudanese villages from Nuer Land
Rok	meaning	Nuer hand made rope for tiding anything

Guon	meaning	one of south Sudanese bird in Africa
Puur	meaning	Nuer Traditional hand made for ding for summer season for Nuer Farmer use
Pat	meaning	Nuer traditional hand made for women use to separate food, for better clearing
Pam	meaning	mountain at South Sudanese in Africa
Row	meaning	one of big mamal in sea call row from one of South Sudanese Lake
Rooɛ	meaning	Nuer traditional hand made for fishing from the Lake by Nuer fisher mind in Sudan
Rɛk	meaning	Nuer fence from Nuer villages at south Sudan
Dɛn	meaning	this is a man call Den from South Sudanese Nuer man
Jok	meaning	this is the man call jock from South Sudanese man Nuer tribes
Den	meaning	Jok a thin that meaning Deng and Jok they are here now
Tun	meaning	Nuer traditional spoon for eating at south Sudanese land
Ton	meaning	egg from bird or cheekiness
Tony	meaning	one of Nuer traditional smoking for older people from south Sudan hand made
Den kene jok cike wa yieer	meaning	Deng and Jock they went to the river
Den kene Jok a thin	meaning	Deng and Jock are here
Den kene Jok cikɛ wa yiɛɛr	meaning	Deng and Jock they went to the river
Thol	meaning	snake from South Sudanese
Thaak	meaning	male cows
Thäk	meaning	one of Nuer hand made for food caring by south Sudanese Nuer women or men
Jok cɛ rɛc nak	meaning	Jock kill the fish
Dɛn kɛnɛ Jok a thin	meaning	Deng and Jock they are here

Dɛn kenɛ jok cike wä yiɛɛr	meaning	Deng kene Jock they went to river
Jok cɛ rɛc nak	meaning	Jock he kill the fish
Wut	meaning	one of Nuer Man from south Sudanese
Luth	meaning	one of South Sudanese fish call luth from one of south Sudanese lake
Kum	meaning	hat any hat for both man or women
Dɛn cɛ guön näk thok yieer	meaning	Deng he kill one bird call guon by the river
Den kene jok a thin	meaning	Deng and Jock they are here
Dɛn kɛnɛ jock cike wä yieer	meaning	Deng and Jock they went to the river
Jok ce rɛc näk	meaning	Jock he kill the fish
Dɛn cɛ guon näk thok yiɛɛr	meaning	Deng he kill the fish by the river
Wan	meaning	one of South Sudanese animal call wan from Africa
With	meaning	one of south Sudanese traditional hand made for men call with in south Sudan
Wuut	meaning	one of the faster running bird from south Sudan call wuut
Dɛn cuɛ guön bul	meaning	Deng his cooking one of the bird by burring it before he eat it
Dɛn kɛnɛ jok a thin	meaning	Deng and Jock they are here
Dɛn kɛnɛ jock cikɛ wä yiɛɛr	meaning	Deng and Jock they went to the river
Jok cɛ rec näik	meaning	Jock he kill the fish from one of the lak in south Sudan
Dɛn cɛ guon nak thok yieer	meaning	Deng he kill one of the bird call guon by the river
Dɛn cɛ guon bul	meaning	Deng he burring the bird call guon by cooking it
Yan	meaning	one of the Nuer cow from South Sudan villages
Yak	meaning	one of Africa animal call yak from south Sudan
Yöa	meaning	one of south Sudanese girl traditional dinning hand made call yoa

Cikɛ wä wic	meaning	the man have gon back to their villages
Dɛn kɛnɛ jok cikɛ wä yiɛɛr	meaning	Deng and Jock they went to the river
Jok cɛ rɛc näk	meaning	Jock he kill the fish from one of the lake in south Sudan
Dɛn cɛ guon näk thok yiɛɛr	meaning	Deng he kill one of the bird from the river
Dɛn cɛ guon bul	meaning	Deng his cooking the bird by burring it
Cikɛ wä wic	meaning	he went to the town or villages at south Sudanese Nuer town
Thäk	meaning	one of the Nuer cow call thäk from south Sudanese villages
Mac	meaning	South Sudanese Nuer gun at the villages in Sudan
Kuan	meaning	one of south Sudanese Nuer food call kuan for them to eat. With hand made
Jok cɛ man dɛɛn kam rɛc	meaning	Jock he give the Mother of Deng fish
Den kene jok a thin	meaning	Deng and Jock they are here
Den kene jok cike wä yieer	meaning	Deng and Jock they went to the river
Den ce guon bul	meaning	Deng he cook the bird call guon
Cike wä wic	meaning	he went to the town
Jok ce man deen kam rec	meaning	Jock he give mother of Deng fish
Kerker	meaning	one of South Sudanese animal call keker
Lueek	meaning	one of south Sudanese sea food call lueek
Ken	meaning	one of south Sudanese bird call ken
Kueet	meaning	one of south Sudanese tote call kueet
Kew	meaning	one of south Sudanese animal call kew
Den ce man Deen kwm guon	meaning	Den he give Mother of Deng bird call guon
Loc	meaning	one of Nuer traditional stake for holding the cow on the ground. Nuer hand made
Gok	meaning	one of Nuer tribes hand made caring women stuffs other use

Löth	meaning	one of Nuer traditional use on their cow neck. For the cow call thak. For young man use
Man Deen ce rec thal	meaning	Deng mother cook the fish from Nuer villages
Den kene jok a thin	meaning	Deng and Jock they are here
Den kene jok ciek wä yieer	meaning	Deng and Jock they went to the river
Den ce guon bul	meaning	Deng he cook the bird
Cike wä wic	meaning	they went to the town
Jok ce man Deen kam rec	meaning	Jock he give Deng mother bird call guon
Man Deen ce rec thal	meaning	Deng mother she cook the fish for her family
can kel Den kene Jok ke guandien cike wa ruup	meaning	One day Deng and Jock with Deng Father they went to the forest
Luak	meaning	Duom or House for Nuer Cows
Kal	meaning	Fence, During Winter month, most Villages have this Fence around their house in the Villages or in rich Family from Town
Mac	meaning	Gun, that mean Gun it is use safely like here In U.S a criminal can not have. Gun Some thing over there too. Any one who have feeling to kill other can not be allow to care the Gun
Bɛl	meaning	milted, South Sudanese have met lit for Food this is what they defend on in the villages. For their small farmer
Bul	meaning	Drum, for playing, for churches pray or for wedding during marriage where all people will come and play in more Number in the Villages
Bith	meaning	neath sword use for fishing, Young Boy ages 17,0r 18 or even older man use it for fishing when they want to fish in the Lak. Or river Bank

Cuk pini	meaning	this is a one of Nuer Traditions made with the mud for their cooling Drinking Water. You can find this any where in the Nuer Villages for Drinking Water
Ciik pini	meaning	the same thing, Ciik mean there is more then one small spot of Drinking Water
Cäl	meaning	Big fish call Cal In Nuer Language this is a good fish to eat
det	meaning	goat in English But in your Nuer Language Mean det, in it is small or big goat in the villages
dit	meaning	bird in English, any bird it did not matter small bird or Big all they are call dit But some time they have different names, But for now if you see this word dit, in Nuer Language it mean bird in English. Any where from Nuer villages will understand it if you say it
dow	meaning	a little cow from Birth, or small cow which was born about four to six weeks
Dhar pini	meaning	Big caring water for the south Sudanese women, from the river, this dhaar it mean it is biggest water caring which can take about three day or one day for the whole house to drink the water from the dhaar water in Nuer Villages. Cool water. Unclean some time they get sick too because water are not pure
dhool	meaning	a boy, any one below age 18 still a boy. But after 18 years of age then you read to get marriage then you are man. And you are no longer be call a boys, only your families like your mother or your Father some time can call you young boy. Just to make you happy
dhan	meaning	Nuer hand made for their sleeping bed in the villages not all people use it, only if you want it, but some time most of their villager sleep on floors
del	meaning	goat in English some time more people in the Nuer villages have more goats, del mean one goat
Rec	meaning	catfish more then one. You can find this kind of fish all the time in south Sudanese Lake
Göök	meaning	monkey in English
Gumut	meaning	This is another bird call gumut

Gat	meaning	child who did not know how to speak yet
ɣɔ_k	meaning	cows more then one cow
ɣöth	meaning	This is another Nuer hand made for caring food
ɣok	meaning	This is another Nuer hand made for water caring
pil	meaning	This is another Nuer hand made for make special food
Tic	meaning	Nuer House, where all villages sleep in village

Thank
Father
Daniel Gatluak Puot Well
FMR Sudanese American Community President

Gat

Mɛmɛ ɛ gat.
Gat a thing
Gat teͤ tɔjä.
Gat luɛdh tät dɛ.

Gaat mual kɛ.

Gat teͤ nyurã.

Gat jälɛ.

Gat Wɛɛ

Gat kinyɛ waŋ dɛ

Gat dɔɔlɛ töök.

Cäŋ

Kueli

Kuel

Pay

Duel

Tic

Luak

Luak ɣɔk

Daniel Gatluak P. Well

Ciööt Due?,,,

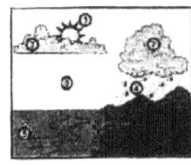

Yär.

Pi yeer.

Piw

Pi̱

Ti̱i̱ ti̱ ke piw mathurä.

Jin gööri piw?

Ɣän göörä piw.

Jin ci math kɛ piw?

Ɣän cä math kɛ piw.

Ɣän ka̱n math kɛ piw

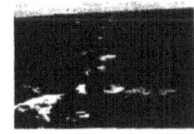

Bäp-diit
pi̱ bäp-diit.

Lööl

pi̱ lōölä

Nhial

Pi Nhial.

Cïöt due------------------

Cäŋ------------------------------------

Man-palëëk

Tuɔŋ

Tut-man-palëëk

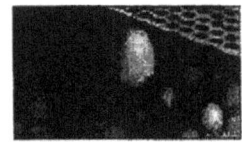

Tooŋ

Man-palëëk kɛnɛ dɛy-kɛ.

Man-palëëk-ni

Gat

Gat kɛl.

Mɛmɛ ɛ gat.

Gat a thin.

Gat ɛ ran.

Gaat

Gaat daŋ rɛw.

Ti ti kɛ Gaat.

Gaat ka thin.

Gaat kɛ naath.

Jin ɛ jin gat?

Gat taa kɛ man

Gat taa kɛ guan.

Gat kwiy ɛ.

Yɛn kɛ yɛn gaat?

Gaat tä kɛ, kɛ man diɛn.

Gaat tä kɛ, kɛ guan diɛn.

Gaat kwiy kɛ.

Tawɛ

Cuk

Dhar

Dhar pini.

Alɛ
Alɛ tha̲t.

Jin Kabi Dhar?
Ɣän kab bä dhaar
Jin kap bi dhar kɛ tät kɛl.
Ceäk kapbɛ dhar.

Jin kabi dhar kɛ tät kɛ ta̲t rɛw
Nyal kabɛ dhar.

Dhar

Mɛmɛ ɛ dhar tha̲t.
Jin ŋäcji tha̲th?

Yän ŋajä thaṯ.
Jin ca ji ŋeeec kɛ thaṯ?
Yän ca vä ŋaaac kɛ thaṯ.

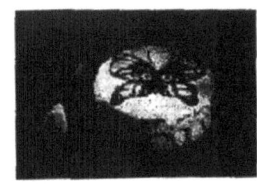

Dɔ-Bul

Kum

Jin ŋäji duäc buɔɔl?
Yän ŋajä duäc buɔl.
Jin ŋ!acji puaṯ buɔɔl.?
Yän ŋacjä puaṯ buɔɔl.

Kun

Thoom

Bul

Jin ŋäc ji puaṯ thoom?
Ŋän kuac jä puaṯ thoom.

Thok Nath/Nuer

Malɛ
> Malɛ Mi gua.

Mal Puɔny Du?
> Ɣän Mal Puɔny dä.

Jin a thin.
> Ɣän a thin.

Mal Gaat ku.
> Mal gaat kä ɛ lɔŋ.

Malɛ Kɛ Run-waŋ.
> Malɛ

Malɛ Kɛ cäŋ-däär.
> Malɛ

Malɛ Kɛ thiaŋ.
> Malɛ

Malɛ Kɛ Wäär.
> Malɛ

www.ingramcontent.com/pod-product-compliance
Lightning Source LLC
Chambersburg PA
CBHW060828290526
45792CB00005BB/1843